# Women in Sports

BY SUE BRADFORD EDWARDS

**CONTENT CONSULTANT**
Jaime Schultz, PhD
Department of Kinesiology
Pennsylvania State University

**Essential Library**

An Imprint of Abdo Publishing | abdopublishing.com

WOMEN'S
LIVES *in*
*History*

abdopublishing.com

Published by Abdo Publishing, a division of ABDO, PO Box 398166, Minneapolis, Minnesota 55439. Copyright © 2017 by Abdo Consulting Group, Inc. International copyrights reserved in all countries. No part of this book may be reproduced in any form without written permission from the publisher. Essential Library™ is a trademark and logo of Abdo Publishing.

Printed in the United States of America, North Mankato, Minnesota
032016
092016

Cover Photos: iStockphoto; Shutterstock Images
Interior Photos: Jeff Bottari/Zuffa LLC/Zuffa LLC/Getty Images, 4–5; Charles Dharapak/AP Images, 6–7; Debby Wong/Shutterstock Images, 11; Pete Niesen/Shutterstock Images, 12–13; Rosseforp/ImageBROKER/Glow Images, 14–15; Everett Collection/Newscom, 18; Minnesota Historical Society/Corbis, 20–21; Bettmann/Corbis, 23, 45; Marty Lederhandler/AP Images, 24–25; Stuart Ramson/AP Images, 28; AP Images, 29, 36–37, 40–41; Ed Ford/AP Images, 31; Paul Walters Worldwide Photography Ltd./Heritage Images/Glow Images, 32–33; Suzanne Vlamis/AP Images, 38; Shutterstock Images, 44, 48, 61, 74–75, 91; Reed Saxon/AP Images, 47; Rob Stapleton/AP Images, 50–51; Rob Griffith/AP Images, 52–53; Mark Shearman/Action Plus/Icon Sportswire, 55; Adam Nadel/AP Images, 57; Pierre Gleizes/AP Images, 59; Lionel Cironneau/AP Images, 60; Julio Cortez/AP Images, 62–63; Han Guan Ng/AP Images, 66; Mai Techaphan/Shutterstock Images, 67; Armando Franca/AP Images, 68; Jim Owens/Community Press/Icon Sportswire, 70; Alison Wright/Corbis/Nomad/Glow Images, 72–73; Mitch Gunn/Shutterstock Images, 77; Dmitry Lovetsky/AP Images, 81; Nati Harnik/AP Images, 82–83; Lev Radin/Shutterstock Images, 85; Hasan Sarbakhshian/AP Images, 86–87; David Allio/Icon Sportswire/AP Images, 89; Lenny Ignelzi/AP Images, 92; Gilbert Lundt/TempSport/Corbis, 95

Editor: Mirella Miller
Series Designer: Maggie Villaume

Cataloging-in-Publication Data
Names: Edwards, Sue Bradford, author.
Title: Women in sports / by Sue Bradford Edwards.
Description: Minneapolis, MN : Abdo Publishing, [2017] | Series: Women's lives in history | Includes bibliographical references and index.
Identifiers: LCCN 2015960357 | ISBN 9781680782950 (lib. bdg.) | ISBN 9781680774894 (ebook)
Subjects: LCSH: Women athletes--Juvenile literature. | Women in the professions--Juvenile literature.
Classification: DDC 796--dc23
LC record available at http://lccn.loc.gov/2015960357

# Contents

Ronda Rousey was a strong advocate for women earning their place in the UFC.

# CHAPTER ONE

# Women Pack a Punch

Two athletes stand on opposite sides of the Ultimate Fighting Championship (UFC) Octagon in February 2015. Fists up, Ronda Rousey bounces on the balls of her feet. When the referee calls the start of the fight, Rousey moves forward—but not as fast or far as her opponent, Cat Zingano. Zingano is normally a slow starter, taking her time to feel out her adversary. But this time, she rushes Rousey and kicks up her knee, ready for a throw.

Rousey bounces to one side and wraps her arm around Zingano's head and neck. Then she throws her opponent down, flipping herself so she cartwheels over Zingano. Rousey pulls Zingano into the cartwheel, trapping Zingano's outstretched arm between her thighs. Bending and overextending Zingano's arm, Rousey has captured her opponent in an armbar.

Only 11 seconds into the fight, Zingano taps on the mat in surrender. At 14 seconds, the referee calls it and the fight is over. Rousey bounces to her feet, cheering in victory. This was the shortest title fight in the history of the UFC. It also tied the record for a submission.

When the UFC was organized in 1993, it featured only male fighters. Female athletes have competed within the organization since 2013. In less than two years, a female fighter had broken the record for fastest title bout.[1]

The UFC offers martial artists an opportunity to compete as paid professionals. UFC fighters use a variety of martial arts, including karate, jujitsu, sumo, wrestling, boxing, kickboxing, and other styles of combat. Unlike the members of many other athletic clubs, UFC athletes must master several different arts to excel because they are not matched according to art. Someone trained in judo may fight a boxer. Because of her background, Rousey uses judo techniques including sweeps and hip tosses against her UFC opponents.

## JUDOKA GREATNESS

Before she was a UFC fighter, Ronda Rousey was a judoka, an expert in judo. In 2007, she won a silver medal at the Judo World Championship tournament. She was the first US woman in 12 years to win a medal.[2] Afterward, she won a gold medal in the 2007 Pan American Games. In 2008, she won an Olympic bronze medal in judo. This made her the first US athlete to win an Olympic medal in judo.[3] It took an athlete with serious skills to open the UFC to female fighters.

UFC athletes can win a match in three different ways. The first is by knockout, in which a competitor leaves his or her opponent unable to continue. The second is by submission, the way in which Rousey beat Zingano.

In a submission, the athlete puts his or her opponent in a painful hold and forces them to give up. Third, in a match where neither fighter is knocked out or submits, the judges choose the victor.

Weight classes divide athletes, so they compete against other athletes of comparable size and strength. Female athletes can fight in only one UFC weight class. This is the Women's Bantamweight, which includes fighters from 125 to 135 pounds (57 to 61 kg).

## NO WOMEN ALLOWED

In January 2011, UFC president Dana White made a clear statement. Women would never fight in the UFC. He did not think there were enough women fighters. But Rousey's athletic ability convinced him to give women a chance to compete. White signed Rousey to fight for the UFC in November 2012. Her first bout was in February 2013.

Rousey is more than a UFC star. She is an actress, an author, a model, and also the woman who convinced the UFC to add a class for female athletes. UFC president Dana White crowned Rousey as the first Women's Bantamweight champion. Her defeat of Zingano was her fifth title defense. Rousey had taken out ten opponents in the first round, nine via armbar, before an upset loss in November 2015 against Holly Holm.

## Women Competing Worldwide

Female athletes excel in a wide variety of sports ranging from rock climbing to mountain biking. Some take part in sports for fun, but many of them join teams. Young athletes can often find teams and leagues to help them learn their sport. Some city swim leagues accept swimmers younger than eight years old and help them hone their strokes. Girls sign up for peewee league football, playing on teams made up mostly of boys.

Teachers and principals encourage athletes to play on high school teams. Schools want their students to play sports because student athletes have better grades, miss less school, and graduate at a higher rate than nonathletes. Student athletes learn to lead and how to be part of a team. As adults, they are ready to become good citizens.

The top sports for female athletes in high school are track and field, basketball, and volleyball. Not all sports have boys' and girls' teams since there may not be enough girls participating in a sport to form teams that can compete against each other. Athletic departments sometimes solve this problem by placing female athletes, especially wrestlers, on the same team as the boys. Female athletes then wrestle boys and girls in their weight class.

## THE PREACHER'S DAUGHTER

Holly Holm, nicknamed "The Preacher's Daughter," tried gymnastics, soccer, swimming, and diving before getting hooked on boxing and kickboxing. As a boxer, she has 33 wins and two losses.[4] In boxing, fighters punch with their hands, attempting to knock out their opponents. Kickboxing adds the kicks used in karate to these punches. Holm used her ability to land a blow on Rousey and win the UFC championship.

Talented athletes who attend US colleges compete on college teams. Some receive scholarship money to do so. Full-ride scholarships completely pay for a student athlete's college education, but partial scholarships are more common.

The very best female athletes perform in global competitions. The most well-known of these competitions is the Olympic Games. Athletes can also compete in various world championships such as the World Indoor Championships, which is sponsored by the International Association of Athletic Federations and features track and field events.

There are also female athletes who play sports professionally, making money through competition. These women drive race cars and ride in horse races. They play basketball and hockey. But not all women worldwide have these opportunities.

## SPORTS AND MODEST DRESS

Women in countries with modesty laws find these laws a barrier to competing in sports. Modesty laws often dictate how a woman should dress. They forbid clothes that are too tight or reveal too much skin, and they may also require a woman to cover her hair. In the 2012 Olympic Games, the Saudi Arabian Olympic Committee said 16-year-old Wojdan Shaherkani could compete in judo only if she wore a hijab. Judo's governing body worried the hair covering would be dangerous during the grapples and tumbles common to judo, but finally agreed to permit the heavy black scarf worn tightly around her head.

# Working for Women

Societies where women are empowered tend to have the largest numbers of women participating in sports. Women must have access to transportation to travel to the stadium, pool, or

Danica Patrick is one of the most well-known
female race car drivers.

Participation in the Olympics by female athletes is common now thanks to many people who pushed for equal rights.

field. They also need time, money, and freedom to participate. Not all countries have granted equal rights to women.

In 1978, the United Nations Educational, Scientific and Cultural Organization (UNESCO) wrote the International Charter of Physical Education and Sport. This document states, "One of the essential conditions for the effective exercise of human rights is that everyone should be free to develop and preserve his or her physical, intellectual, and moral powers, and that access to physical education and sport should consequently be assured and guaranteed for all human beings."[5]

The link between playing sports and learning to lead—as well as learning tolerance and respect for others—is so strong that promoting sports among women was added to the International Olympic Committee's Olympic Charter in 2007. Female participation in sports also helps challenge the idea that women are not capable or should not compete. Female athletes in the Olympics and in the Octagon show the world there is nothing women cannot do, despite the fact that at one time people thought physical activity would harm women.

## OLYMPIC OPPORTUNITIES

The International Olympic Committee tries to promote sports among women. It does this by working to increase the number of opportunities for female athletes to take part in the games. New additions to the Olympic program, such as beach volleyball, must include events for female athletes. If there are not opportunities for women, the sport will not be added.

Croquet was considered a safe activity for women in the 1920s.

# CHAPTER TWO

# Good Girls versus Strong Athletes

For centuries, doctors and many other people in the Americas and Europe believed women were too weak physically and emotionally to play sports. They especially believed this about endurance sports such as running or swimming. Poor women might work hard in a field or a factory, but doctors said wealthy and middle-class women were not capable of vigorous physical activity. Throughout the 1920s, doctors warned women that excessive physical activity would interfere with their menstruation and cause their reproductive organs to harden or die.

Many women avoided sports, but others ignored these concerns and took part in the sports they enjoyed. They played golf, tennis, and basketball. They raced cars, boxed, and swam. Those who had the money to pay the fees joined athletic clubs, and some of these women made it to the Olympics.

One of these women was swimmer Gertrude Ederle, who was born in New York City in 1905. Ederle was a champion swimmer by her teens and competed in the 1924 Olympics. She won a total of three medals, including a gold medal for her part in the freestyle 4×100-meter relay.

In 1925, Ederle started training to swim the English Channel, a 21-mile (34 km) stretch of frigid water between England and France.[1] Ederle would need to combine her swimming skills with endurance and a strong will to meet her goal. Her 1925 attempt to make the swim ended in failure when someone from the escort boat reached out and touched her after thinking she might be drowning.

In 1926, she tried to swim the English Channel again. In addition to wearing her swimsuit, cap, and goggles, she coated her body with grease to stay warm and keep from getting stung by jellyfish. Ederle set out from France and reached the English shore 14 hours and 31 minutes later.[2] She not only was the first woman to swim the channel but also had cut more than two hours from the times of the men who preceded her. Asked about her accomplishment, Ederle said, "I just knew it could be done, it had to be done, and I did it."[3]

Back in New York City, Ederle was greeted by crowds and thrown a ticker tape parade, with paper ribbons streaming down from skyscraper windows. A 1933 back injury ended her competitive career, but she continued to teach young swimmers. Ederle and other gutsy athletes throughout the 1920s took to their various sports to show the world what strong women could do.

# Charm Trumps Athleticism: The 1930s

According to doctors and medical reporters, sports were more than unhealthy. In 1930, a reporter for the *American Mercury* magazine claimed that sporty women "act like men, talk like men, and think like men."[4] A manly woman would have a hard time finding a husband. This mattered because society told women they should stay at home.

During the 1930s, the United States was in the Great Depression. This was the worst economic downturn in the history of the country. By 1933, nearly half of the banks in the United States had failed and between 13 and 15 million people were unemployed.[5] Politicians and other people worked to find more jobs for the unemployed. They encouraged women to leave the workforce and the athletic field to men.

High school physical education programs separated girls from boys. Boys took part in

## FRAGILE FLOWERS OR OLYMPIC ATHLETES?

Before she swam the English Channel, Ederle was part of the US Olympic swim team in 1924. Ederle was one of four swimmers to win the gold medal in the 4×100-meter freestyle relay, and she also won bronze medals in the 100-meter and 400-meter individual freestyle.

Winning these medals was no small accomplishment. The women on the US team were exhausted because they had to travel five or six hours each day into Paris, France, where the Olympics were being held. The US Olympic Committee worried about exposing the female athletes to the alcohol and drug use they thought were common in Paris. Because of this worry, the women were not housed with the male athletes near the Olympic facility.

Mitchell could throw tricky pitches, such as sinkers.

athletics. Girls were active but learned dance, rhythmic movement, and less competitive sports. Educators believed this division took advantage of girls' and boys' natural abilities.

In spite of these attitudes, female athletes such as Jackie Mitchell continued to play and compete. Her father, a sports enthusiast, encouraged his daughter to swim and play baseball. One of her childhood neighbors was pitcher Dazzy Vance.

In 1931, Mitchell went to a baseball training school in Atlanta, Georgia, where a baseball scout spotted the left-handed pitcher. This scout was president of the Chattanooga Lookouts, a minor league team, and he was looking for ways to sell more tickets. His previous tactics included raffling off a turkey and staging an elephant hunt, with men dressed up as elephants and hunters on the ball field. He thought fielding a female pitcher would bring in fans, so he made Mitchell an offer. Seventeen-year-old Mitchell signed the contract to play with the Lookouts. Her mother traveled with her as her chaperone.

Mitchell's first game was an exhibition game against the New York Yankees. As an exhibition, it did not count toward the team's statistics or league standing, but it gave fans the chance to see the team play. Some people believe the events that were said to have followed did not happen. Mitchell supposedly struck out two baseball greats, Babe Ruth and Lou Gehrig. Many people think this game and the strikeouts were another publicity stunt. They did not believe a girl could strike out two legendary players in one inning. Yet other people who saw the game were convinced.

After the exhibition game, Mitchell continued to suit up for the Lookouts and traveled extensively with the team throughout the spring. She then played with another men's team, The House of David, before retiring from baseball in 1937. Her retirement came shortly before women's baseball took off.

## NO GOLD FOR THE GIRLS

Women were not allowed to compete in the first modern Olympic Games in 1896. When asked about women's participation, Olympic founder Baron Pierre de Coubertin said a woman's reproductive system was not "cut out" to withstand the shock of this kind of physical activity.[6] Athletic girls, according to Coubertin, would not be able to have children. Fortunately, not everyone agreed with him, and when it was time for the 1900 Olympic Games, women competed in tennis, sailing, croquet, equestrian events, and golf.

# Batter Up!

From 1941 to 1945, the United States fought in World War II. When men entered the military, they left behind their jobs on farms, in factories, and in sports. As more and more baseball players entered the military, Philip K. Wrigley, Chicago Cubs owner and chewing gum magnate, made plans to create a league of female softball players. He founded the All-American Girls Professional Baseball League (AAGPBL) in 1943.

The AAGPBL scouted players from the women's amateur softball leagues that had grown throughout the early 1940s. Some aspects of the AAGPBL were similar to softball. The ball was closer to the size of those used in softball. In addition, pitchers had to throw the ball underhand. Female athletes, excited at the opportunity to play baseball, signed on to play for teams including the Milwaukee Chicks, the Fort Wayne Daisies, and the Rockford Peaches.

## MS. MANAGER

Effa Manley was the only female owner in the history of Negro Leagues baseball. This league was formed in 1920 to give black athletes an opportunity to play baseball, since they were not allowed to play in the major or minor leagues. Manley and her husband, Abe, owned the Newark Eagles. She handled the majority of management tasks herself, dealing with contracts and travel schedules, and was known among fellow owners for her ability to promote her team. In 1946, the Eagles won the Negro League World Series, beating the favored Kansas City Monarchs. Before her death, Manley wrote letters pushing to have important Negro League players inducted into the Baseball Hall of Fame. In 2006, this hardworking, savvy manager herself became the first woman inducted into the Hall of Fame.[7]

The organizers, including Wrigley, worried about making the athletes appear manly. To avoid this, AAGPBL athletes had to wear lipstick and short skirts unsuited to sliding into bases when playing. Off the field, they were forbidden to wear pants and had to take charm classes, polishing their manners and learning to behave like ladies.

The league recruited and developed top-notch players including Sophie Kurys, who played second base, pitcher Jean Faut, and Dorothy Kamenshek, who played first base. Kamenshek grew up in Cincinnati, Ohio, where she played in a girls' softball league. Scouted by the AAGPBL, she played first base for the Rockford Peaches from 1943 to 1953. Former New York Yankee Wally Pipp said she was the best player, male or female, he had ever seen. In 1950, a scout from a Florida international league team tried to recruit her. But she wanted to play ball, not be a publicity stunt for a men's team, so she turned him down. A back injury ended her career in 1953. She then became a physical therapist and worked with children with disabilities.

The AAGPBL was a hit with fans who wanted to see professional baseball. League attendance grew from 259,000

### GENERAL SLOCUM

On June 15, 1904, the inability to swim cost a large number of women their lives. That morning, 1,350 people boarded the steamship *General Slocum*, an excursion steamer that took people on daylong trips. Ninety percent of the passengers were women and children on an end-of-school outing.[8] When fire broke out belowdecks, the captain beached the ship. Passengers were trapped at the end of the ship, which was 40 to 60 feet (12 to 18 m) from shore. In trying to escape the fire, they jumped into water that was 10 to 30 feet (3 to 9 m) deep. Because they did not know how to swim, between 400 and 600 passengers lost their lives.[9]

Kamenshek, *center*, was such a good player, some people expected her to be recruited by a men's major league team.

in 1944 to 754,000 in 1946, and nearly one million in 1948, when the league peaked.[10] The league continued until 1954, but it was never as popular as it was in its early years. The AAGPBL marked the beginning of women's professional sports in the United States. From Ederle to the women of the AAGPBL, female athletes played hard and showed detractors that women could be champion athletes.

Althea Gibson helped popularize tennis and golf, two growing sports among women in the 1950s.

# CHAPTER THREE

# The Battle to Play in the 1950s

Throughout World War II, women had shown they could do men's work both in the factory and in sports. But as soon as the war was over, society expected women to return to their old roles. Popular writers and psychologists had harsh words for women who wanted to work, describing them as lost, riddled with guilt, and filled with hate for men. Early 1950s television shows and children's books, such as the Dick and Jane series, showed acceptable men's roles—the stern, caring father and breadwinner— and acceptable women's roles—the loving wife, mother, and housekeeper.

During the 1950s, the US middle class grew. These people were not the manual laborers in factories or on farms, nor were they the upper class with yachts, horses, and mansions. The middle class included people who worked in offices, department stores, and a wide variety of government jobs.

Women took part in many sports in the 1950s. Some sports, such as bowling, softball, and roller derby, were considered working class. But the sports that gained the most ground throughout the 1950s were often those that reflected the country-club, upper-class lifestyle the middle class sought to copy.

## Upper-Class Athletics

One of the country-club sports that thrived during the postwar boom was tennis. The top player of the 1950s was Margaret Osborne duPont. But even as country-club sports thrived, the athletes playing tennis expanded beyond the Caucasian upper class. One of the most noteworthy tennis players during the 1950s was Althea Gibson.

### WINNING WAYS

Margaret Osborne duPont was the top-ranked woman in tennis from 1947 to 1950. She was known for being an aggressive player with excellent stamina. Although women at this time most often competed in skirts, duPont insisted on wearing shorts. She interrupted her career once in 1947 to get married and again in 1952 when she gave birth to her son. After giving birth, she made a name for herself when she returned to tennis and continued to win. Throughout her career, she won 20 Grand Slam doubles titles with Louise Brough.[1] A Grand Slam title is earned by winning the world's most prestigious tennis events—the Australian Open, the French Open, Wimbledon, and the US Open. Martina Navratilova and Pam Shriver later tied this record in 1989.

Gibson grew up in New York City's Harlem neighborhood, where she played tennis as a child within the New York Police Athletic League. Sponsored by the New York City police department, the league gives children living in the city a safe place to play sports.

In 1942, as a teenager, Gibson won her first tournament. She was sponsored by the American Tennis Association, an organization of African-American players. Gibson followed this win with the women's singles title in 1947, which she held for ten consecutive years.[2] Her success opened doors that had previously been closed to African-American athletes.

In 1951, Gibson became the first black tennis player invited to the Wimbledon tournament in the United Kingdom. Although she did not win, her game continued to improve and she became known for strong serves and an athletic game. In the 1957–1958 season, Gibson won the Wimbledon women's singles and doubles titles. She was the first black player to win at Wimbledon.[3] Gibson was so popular the Associated Press voted her the female athlete of the year in both 1957 and 1958. She was the first black athlete to receive this honor. In 1971, she was elected to the International Tennis Hall of Fame.

Gibson didn't limit her efforts to tennis. She was also the first black woman to compete in professional golf. For many young athletes, Gibson represented the possibilities of women's sports in general and tennis in particular.

## Women's Golf

The second country-club sport to increase in popularity during the 1950s was golf. A number of women's golf tournaments had been organized in the mid- to late 1940s, and the popularity of these

### AMERICAN TENNIS ASSOCIATION

Founded in 1916, the American Tennis Association (ATA) gave African-American athletes an opportunity to compete against each other on the tennis court. Ora Washington grew up in Philadelphia, Pennsylvania. She held the ATA ladies title from 1929 to 1936. She was a highly skilled player. Some years she did not lose a single tennis match. Because of her success and popularity, public tennis courts were built in many black neighborhoods, giving young players a chance to develop their skills.

Eight of the LPGA founders reunited in 2000 for the organization's fiftieth year.

events led to the organization of the Ladies Professional Golf Association (LPGA) in 1950. Thirteen female golfers, including Babe Didrikson Zaharias, who was known for her talent in several different sports including golf and track, organized the LPGA.

To help the sport become more popular, the LPGA organized the Weathervane series of tournaments. This series consisted of four tournaments, each offering a $3,000 prize with an additional $5,000 grand prize offered for the overall winner of the series.[4]

To truly become popular, athletes needed more than professional opportunities to play. The sport also needed to attract and develop new, talented players. To help developing golfers, the LPGA organized its Teaching Division in 1959 under Shirley Spork, Barbara Rotvig, Betty Hicks, and Marilynn Smith. Golfers in the Teaching Division not only improved their own skills on the golf course but also

# Babe DidriksonZaharias

(1911-1956)

Babe Didrikson Zaharias of Port Arthur, Texas, was an accomplished athlete. She figure skated, dived, and played baseball and basketball. In the 1932 Olympics, she won gold medals in javelin and hurdles and a silver medal in the high jump. In the high jump, athletes get three attempts per height. Most athletes used the scissors kick, kicking up one leg and then the other. For her highest jump, Didrikson performed a Western roll, rolling over the bar on her side. This jump was disqualified but would have won the gold. After her Olympic victories, one sports writer called her "the most talented athlete, male or female, ever developed in our country."[5]

Didrikson began golfing for fun in 1932 and was soon competing in tournaments. From 1948 to 1951, she was the leading money winner among female golfers. In 1950, she and her husband, wrestler George Zaharias, helped found the LPGA. She was diagnosed with cancer in 1953 and eventually died of the disease in 1956. Didrikson serves as an example to young athletes who choose to compete in several sports instead of focusing on only one.

learned to teach more effectively. These athletes held clinics and classes and reached out to physical education teachers, seeking to help them develop young golfers.

## Bathing Suit Competition

As much as society wanted female athletes to choose ladylike, high-class sports, not all athletes took this route. Some entered a working-class sport that was experiencing a boom for both male and female athletes—wrestling. Female wrestlers wore bathing suits and tall lace-up boots, a far cry from the outfits worn by golfers and tennis players.

One of these female wrestlers was June Byers. Byers grew up in poverty and entered wrestling in 1944 with the help of her uncle. She saw wrestling as a way to make a living. It took Byers several years to gain the skills she needed to successfully grapple with and throw an opponent. While she was still learning, she suffered defeat after defeat. But over time, she

### RIDING TO VICTORY

In 1951, the International Olympic Committee decided female riders would be able to enter equestrian events and compete against male riders. But not every equestrian event was open to female athletes. Women competed against men in dressage, a type of horseback riding in which the horse performs specific steps at signals from the rider. Female riders were not allowed to compete in jumping, an event in which the rider takes the horse over a series of jumps at speed. Women also could not compete in eventing, a series of contests that includes both dressage and jumping.

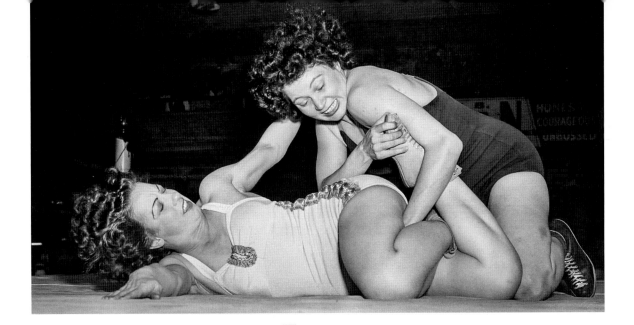

Mildred Burke, *bottom*, was inducted into the
Professional Wrestling Hall of Fame in 2006.

grew to be technically skilled, knowing how to punch, grapple, and throw—and she had earned a
reputation for being a rough wrestler in the ring.

In 1954, Byers entered the ring against Mildred Burke, the women's champion of the National
Wrestling Alliance. Byers threw Burke once, and after an hour of fighting, Burke could not continue
because an old knee injury was bothering her. Byers was awarded the belt, although critics said she
had not actually defeated Burke. Wrestlers such as Byers and Burke inspired fans and young athletes
alike with their showmanship and skill.

Whether they wrestled for a living or played country-club sports such as tennis and golf, female
athletes in the 1950s showed their fans they could not be forced back into the home. Their place was
on the mat, the court, and the green.

Girls participating in sports
through school became more
commonplace in the 1960s.

# CHAPTER FOUR

# Liberating Women

B eginning in the 1950s and into the 1960s, many Americans were changing how they looked at the world and their society. They questioned what was considered fair. Women and minorities had done men's jobs during World War II. Because of this, these people questioned why they were not allowed to do the same jobs in peacetime.

This changing awareness and push for equality led to the passage of the Civil Rights Act of 1964. With this law, public places such as parks, swimming pools, and libraries could no longer segregate people by race. It also became illegal for employers to discriminate based on race, religion, or gender. Although this law did not address discrimination in sports, ending discrimination was on people's minds. Female athletes demanded more and greater opportunities.

# Women Organize

When female athletes asked for more sports opportunities, they did not mean tossing a ball around with friends. To make certain these athletes had access to the programs that would allow them to grow in their sports, the Division for Girls and Women in Sport (DGWS) was created in 1957 as part of the American Association for Health, Physical Education, and Recreation.

The leaders of the DGWS had long known that the best people to understand the needs of female athletes would be fellow women. Within the DGWS, women served as committee members. These committees oversaw the rules and regulation of college-level sports for female athletes.

## ROW YOUR BOAT

As interest in women's sports grew, so did the number of organizations working to improve women's athletics. By 1960, ten colleges offered women's rowing programs, but rowing enthusiasts wanted more opportunities to compete. In 1962, a group of women formed the National Women's Rowing Association. Interest continued to grow, and in 1970 the University of California, Los Angeles founded a crew, followed by Princeton University and Radcliffe College in 1971.

Despite these improvements, many people, often including university presidents and the directors of athletic programs, did not see athletics for women as essential. One DGWS report in 1963 stated women's collegiate athletics were "desirable."[1] Although the DGWS did not call women's athletics essential, athletic opportunities at the college level grew. One of the athletes to take advantage of these opportunities was Wilma Rudolph.

As a child, Rudolph suffered from polio, a virus that can leave a person paralyzed and unable to walk. Rudolph temporarily wore a brace on her left leg, doing physical therapy and exercising until she regained the strength in her leg.

In high school, Rudolph played basketball and trained with Tennessee State University track coach Ed Temple. She competed in her first Olympic Games in 1956, winning a bronze medal in the 4×100-meter relay. She ran track at Tennessee State University and competed in her second Olympics in 1960. In these games, she won gold medals for the 100-meter dash, the 200-meter dash, and the 4×100-meter relay. The Associated Press voted her Female Athlete of the Year in both 1960 and 1961.[2]

Rudolph retired from competitive sports not long after the 1960 Olympics. Working as a teacher and a track coach, she influenced the lives of many young athletes.

## DRIBBLING LIKE A GIRL

During the 1960s, women did not just fight to play. They fought to play the game the same way as the men. During the first half of the 1960s, women's basketball differed significantly from men's basketball. Because some people believed women would not have the stamina to endure a full-court game, female athletes played on a half-court. They could dribble the ball only three times before shooting or passing. In 1966, officials changed the rules to allow unlimited dribbling. Later, in 1969, female athletes played the first official full-court, five-player game.

## Women Making Strides

Even with the work of the DGWS, not every school had a team for every sport female athletes were interested in pursuing. Some of these women took part in club sports, meeting with other members of their club to play for fun. Other female athletes wanted a more serious level of training and competition.

Kathrine Switzer was a journalism student at New York's Syracuse University. This school did not have a women's running team, so she trained unofficially with the men's cross-country team. It was here she connected with Coach Arnie Briggs, a 15-time Boston Marathon runner. When Briggs said it was impossible for a woman to run the marathon, Switzer reminded him that Bobbi Gibb had done it the previous year. Switzer convinced Briggs she could run the marathon by running 31 miles (50 km), 5 miles (8 km) longer than a marathon, in practice.[3] Along with two other athletes from the university, they filled out the paperwork and registered to run the 1967 Boston Marathon. She signed her name as she always did, KV Switzer, without thinking it might hide the fact that she was a woman.

The rules never said women could not run, and none of the officials said anything when she entered the course. Many of the athletes were excited to see a woman running. Partway through the race, Switzer heard the slap of leather-soled shoes on the pavement as a race official tried to run her down. Jock Semple, an official, was determined to get Switzer out of the race. He grabbed at the numbers pinned to Switzer's sweatshirt and nearly pulled her down before another runner from her team, a male football player, slammed into him.

Reporters waited for Switzer at the marathon finish line to ask questions about her experience.

## JUMPING INTO THE RACE

Bobbi Gibb filled out the paperwork to run in the 1966 Boston Marathon, but officials rejected her application. They said this man's race would be too dangerous for a woman. On race day, Gibb wore a hoodie to conceal her face and hid in a cluster of bushes near the start. When the race began, she slipped in among the runners. She worried the men would force a woman off the road or turn her in to the police. But instead, they told her to stick with them. When she overheated and removed the hoodie, spectators cheered. Massachusetts governor John Volpe shook her hand at the finish line. Her entry was not official, but she had run this man's race.

The whole experience shocked Switzer, and she worried the man might be hurt. Relieved to see him uninjured on the press truck, she stuck with the race, finishing with Briggs and one of the other runners on her team in 4 hours and 20 minutes.[4]

Not everyone was as hostile to female athletes as the official who tried to chase down Switzer, and throughout the 1960s, university athletic departments around the country added programs for female athletes. Eventually, a sufficient number of programs had been added that there were enough teams to compete against each other. In 1969, the Commission on Intercollegiate Athletics for Women, a part of the DGWS, announced a schedule for national championships for women in gymnastics and track and field.

## GYMNASTICS GOLD

Wilma Rudolph won Olympic medals and fueled an interest in track. Cathy Rigby created a similar interest in gymnastics as a World Gymnastics Champion. Rigby fell in love with gymnastics when she was a young girl. Her father built a balance beam and parallel bars for her in the backyard of their Los Alamitos, California, home. At the 1968 Olympics, Rigby came in sixteenth, better than any other American before her. Americans admired Rigby's positive attitude and upbeat spirit. Gymnastics quickly climbed in popularity.

Billie Jean King was a star tennis player in the 1970s who set out to prove female athletes were just as strong as men.

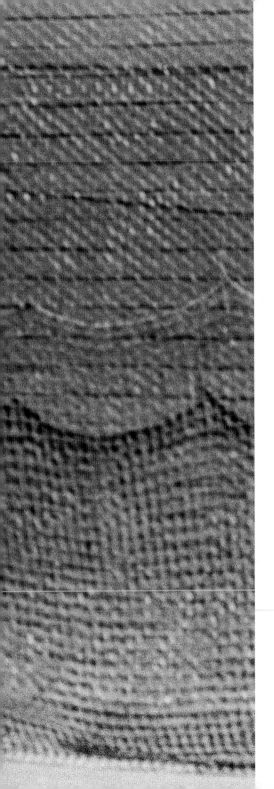

# CHAPTER FIVE

# Title IX: Women's Sports in the 1970s

In 1972, physical educators founded the Association for Intercollegiate Athletics. The organization created policies and sponsored the championships that allowed women to compete against each other. That same year, Title IX of the US Education Amendments of 1972 became a law in the United States. The amendments addressed discrimination, with Title IX focusing on sex discrimination in education.

According to Title IX, no educational program that received government funds could discriminate against girls or women. The law did not address sports by name, but it did impact the hiring of coaches and teachers as well as the purchasing of equipment and facilities. Female athletes had legal support, but it would still take time to change people's minds.

# Battle of the Sexes

After the passage of Title IX, some people said funding women's sports took money away from male athletes. Female athletes knew they deserved this money and had just as much right to compete as male athletes. Tennis player Billie Jean King wanted to show people who did not believe women deserved funding what female athletes could do. Bobby Riggs, the 1939 Wimbledon champion, had challenged King to a tennis match. A self-identified male chauvinist, Riggs had recently defeated Australian tennis great Margaret Court. King worried that if she lost too, it would make many women question what they could accomplish.

King knew Riggs was a showman, so she decided to match his entrance. On September 20, 1973, King entered the court in a couch-like gold litter carried by four men. Riggs entered in a rickshaw pulled by a group of women. King had made a showy entrance, but she took the tennis itself seriously. "Respect your opponent and never underestimate them," she said about the match.[1] King gave the match her all and did not let the huge crowd unnerve her. She won 6–4, 6–3, 6–3. She had soundly defeated a well-known male athlete.

After that match, King had numerous women tell her what her victory meant to them. They knew if she could win, they could stick up for themselves as well. King also had men tell her the match opened their eyes. President Barack Obama told King he was 12 years old when he saw the match, and it has made a difference in how he raised his daughters. Title IX made equality in collegiate athletics the law. King helped people believe it was more than a law. It was the right thing to do.

# Not Playing Around

Because of Title IX, schools had a legal obligation to establish programs for women and girls, but female athletes received less funding and did not have adequate equipment. This happened with the Yale University rowing team during the 1975–1976 school year.

Although the women's rowing team was doing well in competition and the men's team was not, the men had better boats. The men even mocked the female athletes whenever they used the weight room. Each morning, both teams practiced in the icy river. After practice, the men took hot showers in a riverside locker room. The women shivered on the bus waiting for the men to finish so both teams could return to campus. If the female rowers practiced early in the day without the men, they still were not allowed to shower.

The female athletes asked for hot showers but did not receive them even when one of the athletes came down with pneumonia. These women had been admitted to one of the

## BASIC HUMAN RIGHTS

In 1978, UNESCO published the International Charter of Physical Education and Sport. The charter declared that being allowed to play sports and be physically active was a basic human right. UNESCO went on to say schools should develop not only the minds and talents of their students but their physical bodies as well.

# Billie Jean King

(1943–)

Billie Jean King played softball until her parents urged her to try a more ladylike sport. At age 11 she started playing tennis. By her college years, she was known for her speed. In 1971, King joined the Virginia Slims Circuit, a series of tennis tournaments for female players. Because she played and won in this circuit, King became the first woman to win more than $100,000 in tennis prize money in one year.[3] She used her success to lobby for equal cash prizes for women and men. The following year she claimed three major titles, winning the US Open, the French Open, and Wimbledon.

In 1973, she helped form the Women's Tennis Association. The group threatened to boycott the US Open unless tournament organizers addressed the prize money inequality. The US Open became the first major tournament to offer equal prizes to both men and women.

In 1974, King cofounded World Team Tennis, a US professional tennis league. Tennis teams within the league consisted of both male and female players, and, for the first time, women coached male players.

When she retired in 1990, King had won 39 major singles, doubles, and mixed doubles championships, including a record 20 at Wimbledon.[4] In 2006, the facility that holds the US Open was renamed the USTA Billie Jean King National Tennis Center.

most elite universities in the United States, but they could not even take hot showers after practice. Left alone on the bus, they discussed the situation day after day and decided to take action.

On March 3, 1976, 19 women entered the office of Joni Barnett, the director of physical education. The female rowers took off their shirts to reveal what they had written on themselves: TITLE IX. The team captain, reading from a statement, said, "These are the bodies Yale is exploiting...."[5] The women demanded funding comparable to what was given to the men's rowing team. A school reporter took photos of the protest, and the next day the story made the *New York Times*.

As Yale graduates sent checks to help fund the women's team, school officials at Yale and elsewhere realized that to truly

Although Title IX was now law, it would take years for schools to comply with the rules, including Ivy League Yale University.

comply with Title IX, women's teams would need to be adequately funded. Slowly but surely, attitudes began to change in schools across the country.

# Scholarship Funds

One of the earliest beneficiaries of the changes in women's athletics was Ann Meyers, who received a full basketball scholarship to the University of California, Los Angeles, in 1974. She was the first woman to receive an athletic scholarship of any kind to this school. She was also first player, male or female in the National Collegiate Athletic Association (NCAA), to score a quadruple-double. In basketball, this is a player who racks up a double-digit count in four of five categories in one game. The categories include points, rebounds, assists, blocked shots, and steals. Meyers had been a sound choice for an athletic scholarship, but her list of firsts did not end there.

## THE SPARROW FROM MINSK

Title IX was not the only thing fueling an interest in sports in the 1970s. Talented, creative athletes drew others to their sport, as happened with Soviet gymnast Olga Korbut, known as the Sparrow from Minsk. In 1972, she won Olympic gold medals in the team competition, balance beam, and floor exercises as well as silver in the uneven bars. In 1976, she won gold in the team competition and silver in the balance beam. Korbut brought a high level of athleticism and power to this sport, which had previously been about poise and elegance. Korbut even created her own moves on the uneven bars, including a transfer from the high bar to the low bar called the Korbut flip. Korbut's talent and enthusiasm encouraged other girls to give gymnastics a try.

As a college basketball player, Meyers was
the first four-time All-American player.

Meyers went on to become an award-winning sports journalist.

In 1978, she was the number one draft pick in the National Women's Basketball League, and on September 5, 1979, Meyers became the first woman to sign a National Basketball Association (NBA) contract with the Indiana Pacers, a men's team.[6] Although she had excelled in seven high school sports and could play all five positions in basketball, she was only 5 foot 9 inches (175 cm) tall. She had the skills, but if she and another player ran into each other, it was consistently Meyers who went down. She worked hard throughout tryouts, but Meyers did not make the final cut for the Pacers.

Meyers never regretted trying out for the team. The contacts she made with the Pacers led to her work as a sports announcer, commentator, and sports analyst on ESPN, NBC, ABC, CBS, and FOX. And it all started with the expanding opportunities for women afforded through Title IX. Because of Title IX, more female athletes than ever before were able to enter athletic programs and work their way into lasting careers.

## PATSY MINK EQUAL OPPORTUNITY IN EDUCATION ACT

Although many people still refer to the law as Title IX, in 2002 it was renamed the Patsy T. Mink Equal Opportunity in Education Act. Patsy Mink played basketball for Maui High School in Hawaii at a time when female athletes played half-court basketball. Entering college, Mink studied to become a lawyer. After she finished college, she was elected as a state senator for Hawaii. She later went on to represent the state in the US House of Representatives. She worked on legislation that involved civil rights, education, and welfare, and she was the principal author of Title IX. She was still a representative when she died unexpectedly of pneumonia brought on by chicken pox. One month after her death, her colleagues voted to rename Title IX in her honor.

Musher Susan Butcher races up the Yukon in the 1987 Iditarod.

# CHAPTER SIX

# Sports in Bloom

O nce funding flowed into women's sports, the number of female athletes taking part grew. In 1966, 16,000 female athletes played various US college sports. In 1976, that number had grown to 64,000. By 1980, 100,000 female athletes took part in university athletics.[1] Some experts believe growth slowed in the 1980s as schools and athletic programs explored how much support was needed to comply and what government actions would be taken if they did not.

In addition to government actions, schools might be sued. In *Grove City College v. Bell*, a student sued the college to force it to give scholarships to women. The case went to the Supreme Court, where it was decided that any program that did not receive money from the federal government did not have to comply. Privately funded scholarships and athletic programs funded through donations or tuition did not have to give equal funding to women.

Female athletes had to work hard to prove it was worth it to add a women's marathon to the Olympic Games.

This changed again in 1988, when the US Congress passed the Civil Rights Restoration Act. Under this new act, whether or not an athletic program received federal funds, it now had to abide by the rules of Title IX.

# Olympic Glory

While US universities and high schools had to add women's sports, international bodies were under no obligation to do the same thing. Some people believe this is why it was so hard to add the women's marathon to the Olympic Games.

## GOING THE DISTANCE

Part of the reason the Olympic Committee worried about letting female athletes attempt distance running was what had happened in the 800-meter race in the 1928 Olympics. The 1928 Olympics was the first to include female athletes, and this was their longest race. Lina Radke, a German athlete, gave a final burst of speed to win the gold medal with a world record time of 2 minutes and 16.8 seconds. Her record remained unbroken for 16 years.[2] Unfortunately, several runners who had not trained as long or as hard as Radke collapsed at the end of the race. Although this had happened in the past with male athletes, the committee took the collapse of the female athletes to mean women could not run this distance without harming themselves. The committee dropped the 800-meter race from the women's competition and did not reintroduce it until 1960.

Part of the delay was a matter of popularity. The Olympic Committee could not add an event if there were not enough runners to compete against each other. The first international women's marathon was not run until 1973, in Waldniel, West Germany. The following year, the Women's International Marathon

Championship was held in Waldniel. Forty women from seven countries competed against each other. The race grew slowly, and two years later, in 1975, 45 runners finished the race.[3]

Although growing numbers of women ran marathons worldwide, the Olympic Committee was not considering a women's marathon in 1980. Some committee members referred to experts who still claimed women could not run 26 miles (42 km) without damaging their health. The committee would not vote on adding the event until women's marathons were commonplace in at least 25 countries on two separate continents.

By 1981, enough women were running marathons for the committee to vote on whether or not to add a women's marathon to the 1984 games. Kathrine Switzer, who had run the Boston Marathon, championed adding a women's marathon to the games. She kept track of which countries supported a women's marathon and feared the vote would be close. She hoped that persuading one more person to

## MUSH!

Another 1980s first for female athletes came in the Iditarod, the 1,100-mile (1,770 km) dogsled race across Alaska. Libby Riddles raced in the Iditarod in 1980 and 1981. She did not do well in either race but entered again in 1985. Fifteen days into the race, a blizzard forced racers and their dogs to seek shelter in the town of Shaktoolik. Freezing winds still blew when Riddles awoke, but she decided to take a chance. She hitched up her dogs and raced into the freezing wind. This risky move allowed her to establish a lead that she held for the rest of the race, crossing the finish line 18 days, 20 minutes, and 17 seconds after the race began.[4] Riddles was not the only woman to run the Iditarod in 1985. Fellow musher Susan Butcher dropped out when a moose killed several of her dogs. Butcher later won the Iditarod in 1986, 1987, 1988, and 1990, becoming the second four-time winner in history.

Benoit ran the third-fastest women's marathon time ever during the 1984 Olympics.

vote yes would be enough. Before the meeting, she found the Belgian delegate and told him what she knew about the numbers of women running marathons as well as their athleticism and their health. When the committee voted, only the Soviet Union voted against the addition.

US athletes lined up for the opportunity to prove they had what it would take to run at the Olympic level. The US Olympic Marathon Trials was held on May 12, 1984, to select the runners who would represent the United States in this event. There were 267 female runners who qualified for the trials. Of this number, 238 made it to the actual trials and 197 crossed the finish line.[5] On August 5, 1984, one of these runners, Joan Benoit, won the gold at the Olympics. She proved without a doubt

## FLORENCE GRIFFITH JOYNER

At the same time that Joyner-Kersee was winning medals in the heptathlon, her sister-in-law, Florence Griffith Joyner, was earning medals in track and field. Joyner started running when she was only seven years old and at fourteen won the Jesse Owens National Youth Games. She was the anchor for her high school's relay team. In a relay, the last of the four runners is the anchor. Usually the fastest of the four, this athlete is responsible for making up lost time or increasing the lead. After high school, Joyner raced in college. In the 1984 Olympics, she won a silver medal in the 200-meter race and caught the attention of the media. Joyner returned to the 1988 Olympics and won gold medals in the 4×100-meter relay and the 100-meter and 200-meter runs. She also won a silver medal in the 4×400-meter relay. Her speed had improved so much since 1984 that people accused her of taking performance-enhancing drugs. Joyner retired but reminded reporters she had never failed a drug test. In 1995, Joyner was inducted into the National Track and Field Hall of Fame and decided to try out once again for the Olympics. Before this could happen, she died from a seizure. At the time of her death, she held the records for the 100-meter (10.49 seconds) and 200-meter (21.34 seconds) races, which she set in 1988.

that women could run the distance. Not surprisingly, with the inspiration of runners such as Benoit, the number of women running marathons has continued to grow.

## Track and Field

It was not only marathon running that was growing more popular in the United States, but also running in general. As is often the case, one athlete can inspire other athletes to compete in a sport—and in the 1980s, the athlete inspiring others in track and field was Jackie Joyner-Kersee.

Many experts believe Joyner-Kersee is one of the greatest athletes of all time because she dominated the heptathlon. This seven-event competition includes the 100-meter hurdles, the high jump, the shot put, and a 200-meter sprint on the first day of competition. Day two follows with the

Joyner-Kersee narrowly clears the bar during a heptathlon meet in 1998.

long jump, javelin, and an 800-meter race. This combination of events demands speed, strength, and stamina.

Throughout the late 1980s, Joyner-Kersee dominated the heptathlon at the world level. She won the World Championship in 1987. In 1988, she participated in the Olympics and won the gold medal in the heptathlon as well as a gold medal in the long jump.

Joyner-Kersee retired from track in 2001 because of exercise-induced asthma. She then founded the Jackie Joyner-Kersee Foundation in her hometown of East Saint Louis, Illinois. The center encourages young people in this impoverished area to play sports.

## Skating to Glory

During the Cold War (1947–1991), a period of tension between Eastern communist countries and Western capitalist countries, skating often pitted athletes from these countries against each other. The Soviet Union, a communist country, dominated figure skating in the 1960s, and television audiences were thrilled by the athleticism and grace of skaters from the Soviet Union and other communist countries.

Katarina Witt, born in Karl-Marx-Stadt, East Germany, started skating as a five-year-old. When she showed talent, she moved to an intensive sports program at the Karl-Marx-Stadt Sports Club and School. Students at these schools took regular classes and studied their sport. Witt competed in the European and World Figure Skating Championships in 1982 and 1983 before moving up to the Olympics.

Witt drew international attention at the 1984 Olympic Games, beating the favored US skater Rosalynn Sumners for the gold medal in singles figure skating. Witt again won the gold medal in 1988, making her the first woman to win back-to-back golds in this event since 1936.[7] Although Witt no longer competes, she tutors other skaters and mentors up-and-coming talent.

Other skaters chose power over grace, entering the world of speed skating. Speed skaters wear skintight suits with hoods to reduce air resistance. Races are between 500 meters and 5,000 meters long.

Bonnie Blair's father was at a skating competition with her older siblings when she was born. Like her siblings, Blair became a speed skater. Although her siblings all quit, Blair pushed herself to be even faster. In 1984, the 19-year-old competed in her

For most of the 1980s, Witt's technical skill and sense of showmanship ruled figure skating.

Blair races toward the finish line at the
1992 Olympic Games in France.

first Olympics, coming in eighth in the 500-meter race. She kept working, and at the 1988 Olympics she won the gold medal for the 500-meter and set a world record. Eventually, Blair would compete in both the 500-meter and 1,000-meter races. When she retired, she had five gold medals and one bronze medal, more than any other winter Olympic athlete.[8]

Although women were still struggling for funding and support throughout the 1980s, female athletes made inroads into the world of sports. They competed in high school and college, and at the world level they were setting records and drawing fans.

# Dorothy Hamill

Dorothy Hamill first skated on her grandparents' pond with her siblings. She asked for lessons because she wanted to learn to skate backward. Hamill dedicated herself to the sport, often arriving at the rink at 4:30 a.m. to practice. In addition to learning the skills taught by her coaches, she worked on her own moves. One of these was the Hamill Camel, combining a camel, a type of standing spin, with a sit spin.

At the 1976 Olympics, Hamill won a gold medal in the ladies' singles, but competing in the Olympics was not her end goal. "I always knew that I would love to do well enough that I could skate in an ice show, because I always loved the performing part of it," Hamill said.[9] Following the Olympics, she skated in the Ice Capades, a traveling show that combined theater and skating. Families flocked to see her in these shows, and even girls who never skated cut their hair similar to hers in a Dorothy Hamill bob.

(1956–)

One sport that increased in popularity during the 1990s was beach volleyball.

# Dramatic Moments in the 1990s

I n 1991, the NCAA surveyed member schools to determine how well they were complying with Title IX. The organization found that 69.5 percent of college athletes were men; male athletes received 70 percent of all scholarship money; and 77 percent of the budgets for college athletic departments went to men's sports.[1]

Richard Schultz, the executive director of the NCAA, realized member universities had to do better. In March 1992, he established the NCAA Gender-Equity Task Force. The group worked to define equity, find ways to measure it, and come up with ideas on how universities could work toward it. With this renewed effort, the number of women participating in sports continued to grow. This increase was seen not only in college sports but also in high school athletics, recreational sports, and professional sports.

# Beach Volleyball

People have been playing beach volleyball since 1920, but it was not an Olympic sport until 1996, when 18 women's teams from 13 nations competed for medals in Atlanta. The matches took place in a 10,000-spectator stadium, which sold out throughout the six-day event.[2] Supporters say the sport is popular because of the athletes' professionalism as well as the fact that both male and female athletes get to compete.

The winners of the first gold medal for women's beach volleyball were Jackie Silva and Sandra Pires of Brazil. Silva grew up in Rio de Janeiro, Brazil, and she first saw the sport on the city's famous beaches when she was nine years old. She took part in international competitions after less than five years of training. Silva wants to inspire other young people to play and runs an antidrug sports project through the Jackie Silva Institute.

## WHAT IS EQUITY?

As schools worked to improve athletic programs for women, they struggled to define equity. Having as many slots open for female athletes as male athletes was not practical due to the huge rosters required for men's football. The US Department of Health, Education, and Welfare Office for Civil Rights recommended that schools provide opportunities for male and female athletes in proportion to their enrollment. That means if there are equal numbers of male and female students, there should be equal slots for male and female athletes. In 1996, Judge Raymond J. Pettine stated Title IX does not require statistical balance between male and female athletes. He said the school must be able to show there is a history of expanding sports opportunities for female athletes or that the interests and abilities of female athletes are being met.

Pires and Silva teamed up in 1993 and have a winning team, so by the time they made it to the Olympics, most experts expected this winning streak to continue. They did not disappoint, playing their final matches against fellow Brazilians.

## Soccer Spectacular

Another sport that gained popularity in the 1990s was women's soccer. In part, this was due to soccer's international governing body, the International Federation of Association Football (FIFA), creating the Women's World Cup. The first tournament was held in 1991.

The US team dominated the 12-team event, winning every match. Nineteen-year-old Mia Hamm was the youngest member of this team. In 1996, Hamm and several of her World Cup teammates went to the Olympics and won the gold. This occurred in Atlanta, with US fans cheering the home team to victory. In 1999, Hamm was again on the US team when it won a second World Cup.

### TOO MUCH COMPETITION

Women's soccer may not have become popular in the United States until the 1990s, but in the United Kingdom, where the sport is known as football, it drew huge crowds as early as the 1920s. On Boxing Day, the day after Christmas, in 1920, a match between the Dick, Kerr's Ladies F. C. and the Saint Helen's Ladies pulled in a crowd of 53,000 people. Approximately 10,000 disappointed fans had to be locked out because the stadium ran out of space.[3] Almost one year later, the Football Association passed a rule banning women's football throughout Europe. They claimed the game was unsuitable to women and should not be encouraged. Critics accused the Football Association of wanting to divert the women's fans to the men's games. The ban was not lifted until 1971, and attendance still is not as high as it was in 1920.

# Bikini *Ball*

Since beach volleyball made its Olympic debut in 1996, many of the female athletes have worn bikinis. They opted for bodysuits whenever the weather turned chilly. In 1999, the International Volleyball Federation (FIVB) ruled that female athletes had to wear bikinis. Critics claimed the organization was turning female athletes into objects and using them to sell tickets. They said this because male athletes did not have to wear tiny suits.

In 2012, the FIVB backed down. In international competitions, such as the Olympics, players could wear long-sleeved shirts and shorts that almost touched their knees. They made this change so women could compete even if they came from countries where they dressed conservatively for religious reasons.

Reporters asked US athletes if they felt used by the FIVB. "I'm not a sex symbol; I'm an athlete," said Kerri Walsh. Misty May-Treanor agreed. "What you see is what you get—there's no airbrushing," she said.[4] Some athletes claim the two-piece suits are more comfortable. Sand works its way into loose-fitting clothing, where it rubs and itches. The US athletes chose to keep their bikinis.

Conservative countries such as Iraq opt to wear more modest uniforms.

Some teams have chosen to keep their bikini uniforms for comfort reasons.

Hamm became a more confident player and also learned how to deal with failure during her time on the World Cup and Olympic teams.

During this tournament, Hamm scored her 108th goal, setting the record for the most international goals scored. She held this record until June 2013.[5]

Hamm became a media darling whom reporters described as "the biggest US born soccer star of all time."[6] Hamm, who started playing when she was five years old, said that as she worked her way up through soccer to the World Cup and Olympic level, she learned to work with others as part of a team. She now works to encourage other athletes because she wants this same experience for young players.

## The Wonder of Women's Basketball

In 1990, when the NBA sponsored an event for the Women's Basketball Coaches Association, NBA commissioner, David Stern, received 800 thank-you letters. These letters helped Stern realize how many people were involved in women's basketball, and he started working on plans for a women's basketball league.

Before his league could launch, the United States formed the women's basketball USA National Team. The team would play together for a year and hone their teamwork before tackling the 1996 Olympics. The USA National Team started touring in 1995 and won 52 consecutive games.[7]

This winning streak whipped up even more interest in the game. Stern was not ready to launch his league, but a group of businessmen signed nine of the eleven Olympic players to open the American Basketball League. Then the National Team played in the Olympics. With the home court advantage, they won eight out of eight games for the gold medal.[8]

It was into this enthusiastic atmosphere that Stern and the NBA launched the Women's National Basketball Association (WNBA) in 1996. One of the most popular WNBA athletes was Sheryl Swoopes, who first dominated the court when she played for South Plains College in Levelland, Texas. She was voted Junior College Player of the Year in 1991.

Swoopes then transferred to Texas Tech University in Lubbock. In only 46 games at that university, she scored a school

## NETBALL

The game played by the WNBA is familiar to US fans, but another form of women's basketball is popular in other parts of the world. In 1891, when James Naismith invented basketball for male athletes, Senda Berenson Abbott saw the game and created a women's version. She divided the court into three sections with players assigned to each area. This kept them from running the entire court and tiring themselves. Abbott also believed the divided court encouraged the athletes to work as a team. This version of women's basketball is now called netball and is the number one sport for female athletes in Australia, New Zealand, the United Kingdom, and Hong Kong.

Swoopes, *left*, began coaching the
women's basketball team at Loyola
University in Chicago, Illinois, in 2013.

record-breaking 1,000 points. She set more than ten school records, including most points scored per game.[9] In 1993, Swoopes led her team through the NCAA Championships and was named Most Valuable Player of the NCAA Final Four Championships. After college, she played on the USA National Team and made it to the 1996 Olympics, where she helped the team win a gold medal.

Given this level of success, it surprised no one when, in 1997, Swoopes was the first player signed to the WNBA and played forward for the Houston Comets, leading the team to four consecutive WNBA Championships.

## Snowy Thrills

Just as Olympic wins in basketball helped fuel an enthusiasm for that sport, a popular Olympic skier named Picabo Street boosted interest in skiing. Street grew up in Sun Valley, Idaho, a popular ski area. She skied from an early age and joined the US Junior Ski Team when she was only 15 years old. Street trained with the US team, but officials worried about her lack of discipline and poor attitude. They suspended her in 1990. She went to Hawaii to train with her father. Street returned in 1991, stronger and more committed to her sport.

By 1992, Street was listed as eighth in the world. In 1994, she skied in the Olympic Games, earning a silver medal in the downhill competition. This was the same year she became the first US woman to win the World Cup women's downhill competition. She had surgery and physical therapy after a knee injury and came back to win an Olympic gold medal in the 1998 Super G, a run that combines downhill skiing with slalom, weaving between flags. Shortly after this, during the 1998 World Cup, she struck a fence, breaking her leg in several places.

Downhill skiing injuries are often severe because skiers may top 70 miles per hour (110 kmh) before they fall or hit an obstacle. Skiers like Street have surgery and then complete a series of exercises to regain their strength. They must also overcome the fear that often accompanies a serious injury.

Although Street no longer competes, she works with the US Olympic Committee's Stay on the Slopes. The goal of this program is to make sure athletes have the right equipment, know how to use it, and have achieved the fitness level needed to avoid injuries.

## INJURED ATHLETES

Gymnastics continued to be popular throughout the 1990s. Fans eagerly anticipated the performance of the US women's gymnastics team at the 1996 Olympics. The United States had never won the all-around gold medal, but the team was determined that 1996 would be their year. As the games progressed, the chances for a US victory shrank as falls and missteps by various gymnasts cost the team points. It all came down to Kerri Strug and her performance on the vault, an event in which judges take the gymnast's best score out of two tries. In her first attempt, Strug executed a difficult twisting dismount. When she landed, her ankle popped. Reporters questioned if she could vault again with a bad sprain. Fans watched as her coach helped her to the runway. Again, she pounded toward the vault. She stuck the landing and secured the team gold medal.

Whether they competed in professional basketball or world-class soccer, female athletes in the 1990s pulled fans in with dramatic play. They impressed onlookers with their abilities, their professionalism, and their drive to get up and try again.

Girls playing sports is no longer
a rare occurrence in the 2010s.

# CHAPTER EIGHT

# A Woman's Right

Female athletes who played high school and college sports in the 2000s grew up in a world in which people understood the importance of physical fitness. Physically active women are not only less likely to be obese but are less likely to drink, smoke, or use drugs. They take care of their bodies and engage in less risky behavior than people who do not play sports. Women and girls who play sports have fewer unwanted pregnancies. Studies show that women who are active and play sports are less likely to develop breast cancer or osteoporosis, also known as bone loss. Playing sports helps keep women healthy.

But women do not play just for their health. They also enjoy the sports and competing. As more women worldwide compete in a sport, the more popular it becomes.

# Diving Away

Diving combines basic swimming skills with the agility and strength of gymnastics. Divers mount either a platform or a springboard and then dive into the water while completing acrobatic moves. The sport requires both flexibility and strength.

In synchronized diving, two divers perform the same moves at the exact same time. Synchronized diving has been a part of the Olympic Games since 2000, when it was added for both male and female divers. This type of diving is especially difficult to score because judges must monitor the technical components of each dive while noting whether the pair of divers is in sync. Because of this complexity, nine judges work together. Four focus on the individual parts of each dive. The other five focus on whether each diver in the two-member team matches her partner's moves.

Fans eagerly watched the 2000 synchronized diving competition. The favorites to win were the Chinese divers, in part because their country has dominated Olympic diving since 1984. They did not disappoint, as Li Na and Sang Xue took the first Olympic gold medal in the 10-meter platform event.

## HORSELESS POLO

Water polo was invented in 1869 when a rowing team created a soccer-like event to be played in the water. They called it water polo instead of water soccer because in one early version players rode barrels much like polo players ride horses. Women's water polo was added to the Olympics in 2000. The US team barely qualified to play in the games but went on to win the silver medal. The Australian team edged them out for the gold.

Synchronized dives must be
identical and timed precisely.

Russian divers Vera Ilyina and Yuliya Pakhalina won the gold medal in the 3-meter springboard event. Both divers attended college in the United States. Before representing Russia in the Olympics, Ilyina attended the University of Texas at Austin. In 1997 and 1998, she was the NCAA Female Diver of the Year, winning the 1-meter and 3-meter diving NCAA Championships. After the Olympics, Pakhalina became the University of Houston's first individual national champion since 1980, winning the 1-meter and 3-meter springboard events at the 2001 NCAA Championships.

## Water Wonders

In addition to gathering poolside to watch divers, Olympic fans in the 2000s gathered to watch US swimmers power through the water. One of the first US swimmers to draw attention was Maritza Correia, who was born in Puerto Rico and grew up in Florida. Correia's doctor recommended she take up swimming when she was seven years old. She had scoliosis and her doctor believed swimming would strengthen her back. Correia took to her new sport, and by the time she made it to Tampa Bay Technical High School, she was one of the state's top swimmers.

In college, Correia failed to make the 2000 Olympic team. She responded by training harder than ever. She swam six days a week, 14,000 meters (46,000 feet) each day. Her efforts paid off. At the 2001 World Championships, she won a gold medal in the 800-meter freestyle relay and a silver medal in the 4×100-meter freestyle relay. During the 2002 Women's NCAA Championships, she set records in the 50-yard (46 m) and 100-yard (91 m) freestyle events. She became the first African-American woman to set US records in these events.[1]

When Correia made the 2004 Olympic team, she became the first African-American woman to swim for the United States. Shoulder pain forced her to retire, but she promoted swimming as a speaker for the Women's Sports Foundation, where she worked with tennis legend Billie Jean King.

Another swimmer who drew fans was Dara Torres. Torres began swimming at an early age, setting her first national record when she was only 12 years old. She competed in her first Olympic Games in 1984, winning a gold medal as part of the 4×100-meter relay. While attending the University of Florida on a swimming scholarship, she competed in the 1988 Olympics, winning a bronze medal in the 4×100-meter freestyle relay and a silver medal for swimming the freestyle in the 4×100-meter medley relay. After college, Torres swam in the 1992 Olympics, winning a gold medal. Because Torres had graduated from college, she felt it was time to retire from competitive swimming. After sitting out the 1996 Olympics, the drive to compete was back. She once again made the team, and in the 2000 Olympics she won five medals.

## SMOOTH SAILING

In 2005, when the United Kingdom's Ellen MacArthur sailed across the finish line near the French coast, she set a world record for solo sailing around the world. Her time was 72 days, 22 hours, 54 minutes, and 22 seconds.[2] Many athletes make multiple attempts to set a record, but MacArthur did it on her first try. She had completed other around-the-world races with a crew. Sailing solo, she dealt with high waves, icebergs, and gale-force winds in addition to nearly colliding with a whale. When asked if the sport required great strength, Robin Knox-Johnston, the first person to sail solo around the world, said it is not physical strength that is most important. He explained that a solo sailor such as MacArthur has to have amazing discipline and focus.

# Women's Sports
## *Foundation*

In 1974, tennis player Billie Jean King founded the Women's Sports Foundation. The organization's mission "is to advance the lives of girls and women through sport and physical activity."[3] Whether a girl is interested in tennis or soccer, or a woman fences or rides motocross, the foundation wants them to know they are part of a large group of women athletes. Through the foundation, female athletes can receive funds to train or to attend and compete in competitions, such as the Olympic and Paralympic Games.

GoGirlGo! Grants and Sports 4 Life Grants provide money to organizations that bring sports to the lives of girls, encouraging them to take up healthy habits for life. Play Like a Girl! in Frisco, Texas, uses Sports 4 Life money to run a program combining tennis and nutrition information for girls who take part in this after-school program. Virginia Beach Threat in Virginia Beach, Virginia, uses Sports 4 Life money to fund a basketball team and safe place to practice and play. In 2014, the Detroit Police Athletic League allowed 3,300 girls to play basketball and volleyball and participate in cheerleading.[4]

The Board of Trustees of the Women's Sports Foundation is made up of elite athletes such as softball gold medal winner Jessica Mendoza and figure skating gold medalist Sarah Hughes. These women and others like them recognize the many experiences, such as travel and friendship, they experienced through sports and want to share these experiences with other young athletes.

Women's Sports Foundation funds send
athletes to the Paralympic Games.

Reporters questioned whether Torres used performance-enhancing drugs during the 2008 Games.

Torres caught the attention of US swim fans in the 2008 Olympics. Although she was already a winning swimmer, when she won a place on the 2008 team, she became the oldest Olympic swimmer in history and the only US swimmer to compete in five Olympic Games. Sports fans and reporters asked themselves if a 41-year-old swimmer could truly compete. Torres brought home three silver medals in 2008, giving her 12 Olympic medals in total.[5]

The fact that Torres was winning medals as the oldest swimmer in history drew negative attention. Because other athletes had lied about performance-enhancing drugs, Torres understood why reporters would not believe her when she said she was clean. Torres volunteered to be tested by the US Anti-Doping Agency. The tests came back negative, indicating she was not using drugs. Torres retired from competitive swimming but worked as a spokesperson for SwimToday. Through this group, she hoped to convince young athletes to give swimming a try.

### WHY SWIM?

Torres recommends swimming to young athletes for a variety of reasons. First and foremost is that it is a team sport. "You're cheering your teammates on and helping each other," Torres said. "It's so much fun."[6] Unlike other sports, everyone is in the water participating. Swimmers do not get left out. Swimming is also a sport that an athlete can take part in her whole life. "There are not a lot of injuries in swimming," Torres said. "It's very easy on your joints."[7]

# Williams Sisters

Throughout the 2000s, fans flocked to the sports that featured exciting new talent. A pair of talented sisters, Serena and Venus Williams, attracted fans to the tennis courts. Their father, Richard Williams, taught the sisters tennis. He studied books and taught his daughters on the public courts near their home in Compton, California. Williams moved the family to this rough neighborhood to teach his daughters they would have to work hard to get what they wanted in life.

One thing that pulls in the fans is the sisters playing against each other, which they have done more than two dozen times. Their most controversial match occurred in 2001 in Indian Wells, California. Another player told reporters she believed Richard would decide which of the sisters would win the semifinals, and the girls would make sure this happened. Minutes before the match between the sisters, Venus withdrew because of a tendon injury. When Serena came out to play in the finals, the crowd booed, so the sisters boycotted the tournament. Venus returned in 2016.

Still, the pair drew crowds when they played in other tournaments. Between 2002 and 2003, Serena won four consecutive Grand Slam events, beating her sister in the final every time.

## WHEELCHAIR RACING

Chantal Petitclerc, of Quebec, Canada, was not an athlete when, at age 13, an accident left her unable to move her legs. After the accident, she started swimming. Five years later, she had the opportunity to participate in a wheelchair race. Petitclerc finished in last place. But she kept working at the sport and in 1992 raced in the Barcelona Paralympic Games, winning two bronze medals. In 1996, she added two gold and three silver medals, and later won five gold medals in 2008.[8] Fans were not surprised when Petitclerc was inducted into Canada's Sports Hall of Fame in 2010.

Both Serena, *top*, and Venus, *bottom*, have a distinctive tennis style that emphasizes power and athletic prowess.

A Grand Slam is earned by winning at the Australian Open, the French Open, Wimbledon, and the US Open. Serena told reporters that the wins did not come easily. "I'm playing the best player in the tournament. She knows how to play, how to win. She knows all my weaknesses."[9]

Together, the sisters also make a winning doubles team. They have won 13 Grand Slam doubles titles and gold medals at the 2000, 2008, and 2012 Olympic Games.[10] These wins not only draw fans but also encourage young athletes to take up the game.

Sara McMann competed in the World Championships in 2003 before competing at the Olympics.

# Women's Sports Today and into the Future

I n the past 100 years, women have worked their way into many sports. Their most recent victories include sponsored sports, such as auto racing, and contact sports ranging from ultimate fighting to wrestling. Although wrestling was popular in the 1950s, women's wrestling was not added to the Olympics until 2004. Sara McMann became the first woman on the US Olympic team to win a silver medal in wrestling. McMann wrestled because her older brother wrestled. When he needed a training partner, she took the job. McMann continued wrestling in high school and at the university level, even though there were no women's teams.

McMann now urges athletes such as Rousey, in the UFC Octagon, to show that there is no sport that women cannot do. Female drivers are proving the same thing in the world of auto racing.

## Motor Sports

The National Hot Rod Association (NHRA) has become an entry point for women interested in auto racing. Female drivers make their way onto the track through amateur drag racing. In drag racing, two cars start from a dead stop and race down a short, straight track. The most common lengths for drag races are one-quarter of a mile (0.4 km) or one-eighth of a mile (0.2 km). Some people believe there is no skill in drag racing, but drivers must have quick reflexes and know how to handle both front-wheel-drive and rear-wheel-drive cars. In a rear-wheel-drive car, the engine is over the rear axle. The weight of the car is in back, and it has quicker acceleration. Front-wheel drive puts the engine in front and offers better traction. Drag-race drivers have to be able to handle both types of cars at high speeds.

### ESPNW

Although women's sports are increasing in popularity, media stories about women's sports are rare. Studying three Los Angeles stations, researchers discovered that women's sports received only 3.2 percent of airtime.[1] ESPN laid plans in 2010 to create espnW under the leadership of Laura Gentile. Many sports reporters reacted negatively to this plan for a female-friendly ESPN. They saw it as a type of segregation, but Gentile disagreed. "We will be talking about the WNBA a bit more and talking about women's college basketball a bit more," she said.[2] The aim of this new brand is to allow women and girls to feel that ESPN is truly for them.

In a sport where female drivers face off against male drivers, Erica Enders-Stevens has made a name for herself. In 2012, she became the first woman to win a Pro Stock event, the professional level of stock car racing.[3] Stock cars are street cars, the kinds of cars people buy at car dealerships, but are modified for racing.

In 2014, Enders-Stevens beat racer Jason Line to become the first female Pro Stock champion. Before the race, a reporter asked her what it would mean to win. She said she wants to inspire other women who may doubt themselves. "I'm a perfect example of a normal kid, through hard work and . . . surrounding myself with the right people and having . . . a solid support group, that anything is possible. I hope that's the message that comes across to them."[4]

Enders-Stevens continues to show off her strong driving skills with wins against male drivers.

In 2015, Enders-Stevens won nine races, setting a new record for the most races won by a female driver in a single season. The previous record was seven wins. She scored so many points over the course of the racing season that she secured her second championship before the season ended.

Enders-Stevens works hard to be a successful driver. Practicing in a simulator, she reduced her reaction time from 0.36 seconds in 2014 to 0.023 seconds in 2015. Drivers with a lower reaction time start faster and take the lead. Race cars are manual, meaning the driver must shift gears. A driver who does not know exactly when to shift can lose speed, but Enders-Stevens is excellent at shift sequencing. Hard work and determination have built her skills and her career.

Unlike drag racing, which is largely a US sport, Indy or formula racing is global. Indy cars are single-seat and open-wheel, each wheel extending beyond the body of the car. Where drag races are short and straight, Indy races follow either oval tracks or street routes.

US driver Danica Patrick began racing internationally as a member of the Rahal-Letterman team in 2002. By 2005, she had enough experience to become the fourth woman to race in the Indianapolis 500. This is the most prestigious

## FEMALE NHRA CHAMPIONS

When asked who inspired her as a driver, Erica Enders-Stevens named Shirley Muldowney and Angelle Sampey. Muldowney, now retired, is still known as the First Lady of Drag Racing. She was the first woman to be licensed by the NHRA and the first to drive a top fuel dragster. She won 18 NHRA events throughout her career.[5] Sampey races motorcycles in the NHRA and won the Stock Motorcycle Championship in 2000, 2001, and 2002. In 2006, she became the NHRA's winningest female racer, with 40 career wins.[6] Women are not new to the NHRA, but they continue to break new ground.

In 2007, Patrick began racing for
the Andretti Green Racing Team.

Many observers believe Ellis's successes as a coach will help create opportunities for more female coaches in the future.

US Indy race. Patrick came in fourth, the highest finish for a female driver. On April 20, 2008, in Japan, Patrick won the Indy Japan 300, becoming the first woman to win an Indy championship event.[7]

## Behind the Scenes

As women move into the elite ranks of sports, they are also making their way into coaching and managerial positions. On May 16, 2014, US Soccer president Sunil Gulati named the new head coach for the US Women's National Soccer Team—Jill Ellis.

Ellis grew up in England in the 1970s, where there were no teams for girls, so she tagged after her brother whenever he and his friends played. If the boys needed another player, Ellis joined the game. She did not get to play on a team until her family moved to the United States. "It was the first time I put on a uniform," Ellis said.[8] When the coach asked her what position she played, Ellis did not know, but her late start did not slow Ellis down. In 1984, she captained Burke's Robinson Secondary School to the state championship. She earned a place on the women's team at the College of William and Mary in Virginia.

Ellis worked her way up in the world of coaching, first as an assistant coach at the University of Maryland in the mid-1990s. Her first job as head coach came in 1997, when she was given the opportunity to launch the team at the University of Illinois. From there, she moved to the University of California, Los Angeles and began also working with the US Soccer Federation.

As head coach of the US Women's National Soccer Team, Ellis looks at factors that a high school coach does not need to consider. Coaches who work for Ellis scout teams including youth national teams and college teams. Ellis has to put together a team to play not only World Cup but also Olympic soccer. This means finding players who can handle the tense environment Ellis describes as a pressure cooker. Ellis's planning and work paid off. The team won the World Cup in the summer of 2015.

## Empowering Women

Sports are more than just fun and good exercise. They also empower women all over the world. This is especially true in conservative regions where women have traditionally had few rights.

Three groups seeking to help girls and women in southern India are Women Without Borders, the Austrian Life-Saving Federation, and the Austrian Swimming Association. When a tsunami struck the coastlines of southern India in 2004, up to four times as many women as men died.[9] So many more women died because women and girls did not know how to swim and were not fit enough to climb to safety on the tops of roofs or in trees. Because of this, these three organizations are offering swimming lessons for girls and women who live along coastlines around the world. These groups hope swimming lessons will enable people to save themselves in high water, but also help them believe in their value as human beings with the ability to take charge of their own futures.

## THE FIRST TO COMPETE

The first Muslim woman to compete in the Olympics was Halet Cambel of Turkey, who took part in the 1936 Olympics. When the founder of the Turkish republic, Mustafa Kemal Ataturk, encouraged women to participate in sports, Cambel took up fencing. She represented Turkey in the 1936 Games held in Berlin, Germany, and even received an invitation to meet German leader Adolf Hitler. She had her doubts about even attending the Nazi-sponsored games and refused the meeting, giving political disagreements as the reason.

A similar thought process is behind the International Olympic Committee's efforts to see that female athletes from conservative Muslim nations make it to the Olympics. The first Muslim woman to win a medal was Nawal El Moutawakel from Morocco. In the 1984 games, she won the gold medal in the 400-meter hurdles. The second Muslim woman to win a gold medal was Algeria's Hassiba Boulmerka. She won the 1,500-meter race in 1992. Like all Olympic competitors, these women inspire their fellow athletes and women worldwide.

El Moutawakel went on to become the first Muslim woman to be elected to the International Olympics Committee in 1998.

But the Olympics are about more than winning gold medals. Every athlete who makes it to the games has demonstrated determination, commitment, and awe-inspiring spirit. They also stand as women representing their nations to the world. When Sheikha Maitha Bint Mohammed Bin Rashid Al Maktoum, a tae kwon do athlete, became the first woman to carry the flag from the United Arab Emirates in the 2008 Olympic parade of nations, she did so as a Muslim woman representing her Muslim nation.

In 2012, Qatar, Brunei, and Saudi Arabia, all Muslim countries, entered female athletes into the Olympics for the first time. The participation of these women is vital because it not only inspires other Muslim women but also shows people of all faiths what these women can do. Step by step, sport by sport, female athletes are inspiring others and bringing change worldwide.

Whether they are Olympic athletes or playing on their high school teams, female athletes gain confidence and learn cooperation and

## LITTLE LEAGUE BASEBALL

In 1974, the Little League changed its Federal Charter to allow female athletes to play Little League Baseball. It created Little League Softball the same year. Since then, 18 girls have played in the Little League World Series, including two players in 2014: Mo'ne Davis from Philadelphia, Pennsylvania, and Emma March from Vancouver, Canada. Davis is a pitcher and March plays first base. "I believe every girl should have the opportunity to play sports and enjoy it," said March. "Sports are not something you should be afraid of. It should be something that excites you."[10] For these athletes, the choice is baseball.

leadership. Some of them come from athletic families, while others have sporty friends. Still others received encouragement from a teacher or coach.

Fortunately, many athletes are willing to encourage their sisters in sport, whether they do this online or simply by speaking to younger athletes whenever the opportunity arises. It is their way of cheering on those who will make the catches, run the races, and swim the laps that will inspire yet another group of girls to push themselves to go one step further—both in sports and in the global community.

## DROPPING THE PUCK

Dani Rylan grew up a hockey-loving girl in Tampa, Florida, in the 1990s. Her hockey hero was not a male player but Manon Rhéaume from the Canadian Olympic Women's Hockey team. When she saw Rhéaume in the goal for the Tampa Bay Lightning during a preseason game, Rylan thought, "This is awesome. This is possible."[11] She wanted other girls to be inspired by top female hockey players, so she organized the National Women's Hockey League. The league's first game took place on October 11, 2015.

# Timeline

**1900**

Women compete in the Olympic Games for the first time.

**1926**

Gertrude Ederle swims the English Channel.

**1943**

The All-American Girls Professional Baseball League (AAGPBL) is founded.

**1950**

The Ladies Professional Golf Association (LPGA) is organized.

**1958**

Althea Gibson is the first black player to win at Wimbledon.

**1967**

Kathrine Switzer runs in the Boston Marathon.

**1969**

Women first play full-court basketball.

**1972**

Title IX becomes law.

**1973**

Billie Jean King beats Bobby Riggs in a tennis match on September 20; the first international women's marathon is run.

**1974**

Ann Meyers is the first woman to receive an athletic scholarship to the University of California, Los Angeles; Billie Jean King founds the Women's Sports Foundation.

**1976**

Nineteen members of the Yale women's rowing crew stage a protest and demand funding comparable to that given to the men's crew on March 3.

## 1978

The United Nations Educational, Scientific and Cultural Organization (UNESCO) declares access to sports and physical fitness a human right.

## 1984

Nawal El Moutawakel is the first Muslim woman to win a gold medal at the Olympic Games.

## 1991

Soccer's international governing body, the International Federation of Association Football (FIFA), first offers the Women's World Cup.

## 1996

Beach volleyball for men and women is added to the Olympic Games; the Women's National Basketball Association (WNBA) is established.

## 2007

The International Olympic Committee makes promoting sports among women one of its goals.

## 2008

Danica Patrick becomes the first woman to win an Indy championship event.

## 2013

Women are allowed to compete within the Ultimate Fighting Championship (UFC); Ronda Rousey is the UFC Women's Bantamweight champion.

## 2015

The first National Women's Hockey League game is played on October 11.

# Essential Facts

## KEY PLAYERS

- Babe Didrikson Zaharias, the top athlete of her time, gold and silver medals winner for track and field in the 1932 Olympics and the leading money winner in women's golf from 1948 to 1951

- Gertrude Ederle, the first woman to swim the English Channel in 1926 when her time, 14 hours and 31 minutes, set the record for male and female swimmers

- Billie Jean King, the top women's tennis player who defeated Bobby Riggs, a male Wimbledon champion, in 1973 and remains an outspoken supporter of equal pay for women athletes and access to sports for women and girls worldwide

- Kathrine Switzer, the first woman who registered in and ran the Boston Marathon in 1967 and continues to be an outspoken champion for women's marathons and female runners

- Sheryl Swoopes, the first player signed to the WNBA in 1997

## WOMEN AS ATHLETES

As late as the 1950s, women in the United States and Europe were discouraged from taking part in sports. Some doctors said that women simply could not do it—the strain would injure them. Despite this, women swam, ran, and pushed themselves, proving what they could do. The turning point for female athletes in the United States came when Title IX became a law in 1972. With this law, schools that received federal funding for sports had to provide sports for both genders. The law has not been without critics, who claim, even today, that giving money to female athletes means taking money away from men. Regardless, women have continued to fight for their right to compete at all levels.

## IMPACT ON SOCIETY

Playing sports teaches leadership skills and the ability to cooperate. It also boosts athletes' confidence and belief in themselves. Women who do not have access to sports and physical fitness often do not have the ability to move about freely in their own societies or make decisions about their time or money. Access to sports and physical education goes hand in hand with other rights for women. Women excelling in sports encourage other women to do the same.

## QUOTE

"I just knew it could be done, it had to be done, and I did it."
—*Gertrude Ederle on swimming the English Channel*

# Glossary

**CAPITALIST**
Having to do with an economic system where businesses are privately owned and operated for the purpose of making a profit.

**CHAPERONE**
An older person, often married, who accompanies and supervises a younger person.

**COMMUNIST**
Having to do with a system in which the government controls the economy and owns all property.

**DOUBLES**
A tennis match between two pairs of players.

**EQUESTRIAN**
Involving horseback riding.

**FRONT-WHEEL DRIVE**
A system in which the engine powers the front wheels of a motor vehicle.

**MAGNATE**
An entrepreneur or innovative businessperson.

**MALE CHAUVINIST**
A man who thinks women are not equal to men.

**MARTIAL ART**
A form of self-defense or combat.

**MEDLEY RELAY**
A relay swimming event in which each team member swims one part of the race using different strokes.

**MIXED DOUBLES**
A tennis match between two pairs of players in which each pair must have one male player and one female player.

**PERFORMANCE-ENHANCING DRUG**
A drug, such as a steroid, that helps an athlete build muscle faster, run faster, or otherwise compete at a higher level.

**REAR-WHEEL DRIVE**
A system in which the engine powers the rear wheels of a motor vehicle.

## SCOLIOSIS

A lateral curvature of the spine.

## SCOUT

A person whose job is to watch games and look for players to hire.

## SEGREGATE

To separate groups of people based on race, gender, ethnicity, or other factors.

## SINGLES

A tennis match between two individual players.

## SLALOM

A downhill ski course that includes poles through which skiers must zigzag.

# Additional Resources

## SELECTED BIBLIOGRAPHY

"Fact Sheet: Women in the Olympic Movement." *Olympic.org*. International Olympic Committee, Jan. 2016. Web. 5 Feb. 2016.

Pfohl, Shellie Y. "40th Anniversary of Title IX: Status of Girls' and Women's Sports Participation." *President's Challenge*. President's Council on Fitness, Sports and Nutrition, Sept. 2012. Web. 5 Feb. 2016.

Schultz, Jaime. *Qualifying Times: Points of Change in US Women's Sport*. Urbana, IL: U of Illinois P, 2014. Print.

United Nations. "Women, Gender Equality and Sport." *United Nations*. Division for the Advancement of Women, Dec. 2007. Web. 5 Feb. 2016.

## FURTHER READINGS

Douglas, Gabrielle. *Raising the Bar*. Grand Rapids, MI: Zondervan, 2013. Print.

Lobby, Mackenzie. *Babe Didrikson Zaharias*. Minneapolis, MN: Abdo, 2011. Print.

Trusdell, Brian. *US Women Win the World Cup*. Minneapolis, MN: Abdo, 2015. Print.

## WEBSITES

To learn more about Women's Lives in History, visit **booklinks.abdopublishing.com**. These links are routinely monitored and updated to provide the most current information available.

# FOR MORE INFORMATION

For more information on this subject, contact or visit the following organizations:

**Champion Women**
3116 Saint Johns Avenue
Jacksonville, FL 32205
904-384-8484
http://championwomen.org
This nonprofit pushes for women's teams, compliance with Title IX, and equality between men and women in sports.

**Tucker Center for Research on Girls & Women in Sport**
1900 University Avenue Southeast
Minneapolis, MN 55455
612-625-7327
http://www.cehd.umn.edu/tuckercenter
The Tucker Center is a leader in exploring how sports and physical activity affect the lives of girls and women, their families, and their communities.

**Women's Sports Foundation**
1899 Hempstead Turnpike, Suite 400
East Meadow, NY 11554
800-227-3988
http://www.womenssportsfoundation.org
This organization works to improve the lives of girls and women by encouraging them to take part in sports and physical activity.

# Source Notes

## CHAPTER 1. WOMEN PACK A PUNCH

1. Cindy Boren. "Watch Ronda Rousey Beat Cat Zingano in 14 Seconds in UFC 184." *Washington Post*. Washington Post, 1 Mar. 2015. Web. 26 Feb. 2016.

2. "Ronda Rousey." *UFC*. Zuffa, 2015. Web. 26 Feb. 2016.

3. Biography.com Editors. "Ronda Rousey Biography." *Biography.com*. A&E Television Networks, n.d. Web. 26 Feb. 2016.

4. Char Adams. "5 Things to Know About Holly Holm, the Fighter Who Delivered a Surprise Knockout Blow to Ronda Rousey." *People*. Time, 16 Nov. 2015. Web. 26 Feb. 2016.

5. "International Charter of Physical Education and Sport." *UNESCO*. UNESCO, 21 Nov. 1978. Web. 26 Feb. 2016.

## CHAPTER 2. GOOD GIRLS VERSUS STRONG ATHLETES

1. Biography.com Editors. "Gertrude Ederle Biography." *Biography.com*. A&E Television Networks, n.d. Web. 26 Feb. 2016.

2. Ibid.

3. Ibid.

4. Susan K Cahn. "From the 'Muscle Moll' to the 'Butch' Ballplayer: Mannishness, Lesbianism, and Homophobia in US Women's Sports." *Feminist Studies*. Feminist Studies, Summer 1993. Web. 26 Feb. 2016.

5. History.com Staff. "The Great Depression." *History.com*. A&E Networks, n.d. Web. 26 Feb. 2016.

6. United Nations. "Women, Gender Equality and Sport." *United Nations*. Division for the Advancement of Women, Dec. 2007. Web. 26 Feb. 2016.

7. "Effa Manley." *National Baseball Hall of Fame*. National Baseball Hall of Fame, n.d. Web. 26 Feb. 2016.

8. "Report of the United States Commission of Investigation Upon the Disaster to the Steamer 'General Slocum.'" *US Coast Guard*. US Department of Commerce and Labor, 8 Oct. 1904. Web. 26 Feb. 2016.

9. Ibid.

10. Arleene Johnson Noga. "All-American Girls' Baseball League—Its History in Brief—1943 to 1946." *All-American Girls Professional Baseball League Players Association*. All-American Girls Professional Baseball League Players Association, 2016. Web. 26 Feb. 2016.

## CHAPTER 3. THE BATTLE TO PLAY IN THE 1950s

1. Robin Finn. "Margaret Osborne duPont, Tennis Champion, Dies at 94." *New York Times*. New York Times, 25 Oct. 2012. Web. 26 Feb. 2016.

2. "Althea Gibson." *Encyclopædia Britannica*. Encyclopædia Britannica, 2016. Web. 26 Feb. 2016.

3. "Althea Gibson is First African American to Win Wimbledon." *History.com*. A&E Networks, n.d. Web. 26 Feb. 2016.

4. "Ladies Professional Golf Association (LPGA)." *Encyclopædia Britannica*. Encyclopædia Britannica, 2016. Web. 26 Feb. 2016.

5. Biography.com Editors. "Babe Didrikson Zaharias Biography." *Biography.com*. A&E Television Networks, n.d. Web. 26 Feb. 2016.

## CHAPTER 4. LIBERATING WOMEN

1. Richard C. Bell. "A History of Women in Sport Prior to Title IX." *Sport Journal*. United States Sports Academy, 14 Mar. 2008. Web. 26 Feb. 2016.

2. Biography.com Editors. "Wilma Rudolph Biography." *Biography.com*. A&E Television Networks, n.d. Web. 26 Feb. 2016.

3. Tom Jackman. "Kathrine Switzer, Boston Marathon Women's Pioneer, Started Running in Dunn Loring, Went to Marshall HS." *Washington Post*. Washington Post, 23 Sept. 2012. Web. 26 Feb. 2016.

4. "The Real Story of Kathrine Switzer's 1967 Boston Marathon." *Kathrine Switzer Marathon Woman*. Kathrine Switzer Marathon Woman, 2016. Web. 26 Feb. 2016.

## CHAPTER 5. TITLE IX: WOMEN'S SPORTS IN THE 1970s

1. "Billie Jean King: This Tennis Icon Paved the Way for Women in Sports." *TED*. TED, Sep. 2015. Web. 26 Feb. 2016.

2. "Title IX of the Education Amendments of 1972." *United States Department of Justice*. Justice.gov, 6 Aug. 2015. Web. 26 Feb. 2016.

3. Biography.com Editors. "Billie Jean King Biography." *Biography.com*. A&E Television Networks, n.d. Web. 26 Feb. 2016.

4. Ibid.

5. Steve Wulf. "Title Waves." *ESPNW*. ESPN, 14 June 2012. Web. 26 Feb. 2016.

6. Dana Hunsinger Benbow. "Ann Meyers Took Her Best Shot at Making the Pacers." *IndyStar*. USAToday, 4 June 2015. Web. 26 Feb. 2016.

## CHAPTER 6. SPORTS IN BLOOM

1. Shawn Ladda. "Examining Title IX at 40: Historical Development, Legal Implications, and Governance Structures." *President's Challenge*. President's Council on Fitness, Sports and Nutrition, Sept. 2012. Web. 5 Feb. 2016.

2. "Lina Radke." *Encyclopædia Britannica*. Encyclopædia Britannica Inc., 2016. Web. 26 Feb. 2016.

3. Charlie Lovett. *Olympic Marathon*. Westport, CT: Greenwood, 1997. *Marathonguide.com*. Web. 26 Feb. 2016.

4. B. Myint. "Libby Riddles: The First Lady of the Iditarod." *Biography.com*. A&E Television Networks, n.d. Web. 26 Feb. 2016.

# Source Notes Continued

5. Charlie Lovett. *Olympic Marathon*. Westport, CT: Greenwood, 1997. *Marathonguide.com*. Web. 26 Feb. 2016.

6. Biography.com Editors. "Mary Lou Retton Biography." *Biography.com*. A&E Television Networks, n.d. Web. 26 Feb. 2016.

7. "Katarina Witt." *Encyclopædia Britannica*. Encyclopædia Britannica, 2016. Web. 26 Feb. 2016.

8. Biography.com Editors. "Bonnie Blair Biography." *Biography.com*. A&E Television Networks, n.d. Web. 26 Feb. 2016.

9. Biography.com Editors. "Dorothy Hamill." *Biography.com*. A&E Television Networks, n.d. Web. 26 Feb. 2016.

## CHAPTER 7. DRAMATIC MOMENTS IN THE 1990s

1. Shawn Ladda. "Examining Title IX at 40: Historical Development, Legal Implications, and Governance Structures." *President's Challenge*. President's Council on Fitness, Sports and Nutrition, Sept. 2012. Web. 5 Feb. 2016.

2. "Olympic Volleyball." *FIVB*. FIVB, n.d. Web. 26 Feb. 2016.

3. "Team's Highlights." *Dick, Kerr Ladies FC 1917–1965*. Dick, Kerr Ladies FC 1917–1965, n.d. Web. 26 Feb. 2016.

4. Katy Waldman. "American Beach Volleyball Players Explain Why They'll Continue to Wear Bikinis." *Slate*. Slate Group, 27 July 2012. Web. 26 Feb. 2016.

5. Casey Musarra. "Women's World Cup History." *Newsday*. Newsday, 6 July 2015. Web. 26 Feb. 2016.

6. Tom McGowan. "Mia Hamm: The Most Powerful Woman in Football?" *CNN*. Cable News Network, 5 Feb. 2015. Web. 26 Feb. 2016.

7. "Basketball at the 1996 Atlanta Summer Games: Women's Basketball." *SR Olympic Sports*. Sports Reference, 2016. Web. 26 Feb. 2016.

8. Ibid.

9. Biography.com Editors. "Sheryl Swoopes Biography." *Biography.com*. A&E Television Networks, n.d. Web. 26 Feb. 2016.

## CHAPTER 8. A WOMAN'S RIGHT

1. Biography.com Editors. "Maritza Correia." *Biography.com*. A&E Television Networks, n.d. Web. 26 Feb. 2016.

2. "MacArthur Sails into Record Books." *BBC Sport*. BBC, 8 Feb. 2005. Web. 26 Feb. 2016.

3. "About Us." *Women's Sports Foundation*. Women's Sports Foundation, 2011. Web. 26 Feb. 2016.

4. Ibid.

5. Biography.com Editors. "Dara Torres Biography." *Biography.com*. A&E Television Networks, n.d. Web. 26 Feb. 2016.

6. Laura T. Coffey. "Olympian Dara Torres: 'I Leave and Go to Dinner' During Daughter's Swim Practice." *Today Parents*. NBC News, 30 July 2015. Web. 26 Feb. 2016.

7. Ibid.

8. Jeremy Freeborn. "Chantal Petitclerc." *Historica Canada*. Historica Canada, 25 June 2015. Web. 26 Feb. 2016.

9. Victor Mather. "Venus vs. Serena Williams: A Long, Uncomfortable Rivalry." *New York Times*. New York Times, 8 Sept. 2015. Web. 26 Feb. 2016.

10. Biography.com Editors. "Venus Williams Biography." *Biography.com*. A&E Television Networks, n.d. Web. 26 Feb. 2016.

## CHAPTER 9. WOMEN'S SPORTS TODAY AND INTO THE FUTURE

1. Katie Thomas. "ESPN Slowly Introducing Online Brand for Women." *New York Times*. New York Times, 15 Oct. 2010. Web. 26 Feb. 2016.

2. Kiley Kroh. "SportsCenter's Shameful Coverage of Women's Sports." *ThinkProgress*. Center for American Progress Action Fund, 12 June 2015. Web. 26 Feb. 2016.

3. Tony Fabrizio. "How Erica Enders Became the 'Best Driver Ever.'" *ESPNW*. ESPN, 2 Dec. 2015. Web. 26 Feb. 2016.

5. Biography.com Editors. "Shirley Muldowney Biography." *Biography.com*. A&E Television Networks, n.d. Web. 26 Feb. 2016.

6. "Angelle Sampey." *NHRA*. NHRA, 2015. Web. 26 Feb. 2016.

7. Biography.com Editors. "Danica Patrick Biography." *Biography.com*. A&E Television Networks, n.d. Web. 26 Feb. 2016.

8. Steven Goff. "Jill Ellis Played Soccer with Boys. Now She Leads US in Women's World Cup." *Washington Post*. Washington Post, 11 June 2015. Web. 26 Feb. 2016.

9. John Aglionby. "Four Times as Many Women Died in Tsunami." *Guardian*. Guardian News and Media, 26 Mar. 2005. Web. 26 Feb. 2016.

10. "The 18 Girls Who Have Made Little League Baseball World Series History." *Little League*. Little League International, 1 Feb. 2015. Web. 26 Feb. 2016.

11. "Manon Rhéaume to Drop Puck on NWHL Opening Day." *NWHL*. NWHL, 2015. Web. 26 Feb. 2016.

# Index

# About the Author

Sue Bradford Edwards writes nonfiction for children and teens, working from her home in Saint Louis, Missouri. Edwards took dance lessons and ice-skating as a kid. For fun, she hiked and went fishing with her grandmother. Her favorite form of exercise now is yoga. Her books for young readers cover a wide variety of titles including *Ancient Maya, The Bombing of Pearl Harbor, Black Lives Matter, Gertrude Ederle versus the English Channel*, and *12 Incredible Facts about the Cuban Missile Crisis*.